THE SENSE

by the same author

FIGHTING TERMS
MY SAD CAPTAINS
POSITIVES
TOUCH
MOLY
JACK STRAW'S CASTLE
SELECTED POEMS 1950–1975
THE PASSAGES OF JOY
THE MAN WITH NIGHT SWEATS
COLLECTED POEMS
BOSS CUPID

essays
THE OCCASIONS OF POETRY:
Essays in Criticism and Autobiography
SHELF LIFE

The Sense of Movement

THOM GUNN

faber and faber

First published in 1957
by Faber and Faber Limited
3 Queen Square London WC1N 3AU
First published in this edition 1968
Reset in 2001

Photoset by Wilmaset Ltd, Wirral
Printed in Italy

A CIP record for this book
is available from the British Library

ISBN 0-571-21008-2

2 4 6 8 10 9 7 5 3 1

'Je le suis, je veux l'être.'
Auguste in *Cinna*

Acknowledgements are made to the following, in which some of these poems have appeared: *London Magazine*, *Paris Review*, *Poetry* (Chicago), *Spectator*, *Times Literary Supplement*, *Encounter*, *Listen*, *Times Educational Supplement*, *New Orleans Poetry Journal*, *Cambridge Review*, *New Lines*, and the BBC Third Programme.

Contents

On the Move
'Man, you gotta Go.'

The blue jay scuffling in the bushes follows
Some hidden purpose, and the gust of birds
That spurts across the field, the wheeling swallows,
Have nested in the trees and undergrowth.
Seeking their instinct, or their poise, or both,
One moves with an uncertain violence
Under the dust thrown by a baffled sense
Or the dull thunder of approximate words.

On motorcycles, up the road, they come:
Small, black, as flies hanging in heat, the Boys,
Until the distance throws them forth, their hum
Bulges to thunder held by calf and thigh.
In goggles, donned impersonality,
In gleaming jackets trophied with the dust,
They strap in doubt – by hiding it, robust –
And almost hear a meaning in their noise.

Exact conclusion of their hardiness
Has no shape yet, but from known whereabouts
They ride, direction where the tires press.
They scare a flight of birds across the field:
Much that is natural, to the will must yield.
Men manufacture both machine and soul,
And use what they imperfectly control
To dare a future from the taken routes.

It is a part solution, after all.
One is not necessarily discord
On earth; or damned because, half animal,

[1]

One lacks direct instinct, because one wakes
Afloat on movement that divides and breaks.
One joins the movement in a valueless world,
Choosing it, till, both hurler and the hurled,
One moves as well, always toward, toward.

A minute holds them, who have come to go:
The self-defined, astride the created will
They burst away; the towns they travel through
Are home for neither bird nor holiness,
For birds and saints complete their purposes.
At worst, one is in motion; and at best,
Reaching no absolute, in which to rest,
One is always nearer by not keeping still.

California

The Nature of an Action

I

Here is a room with heavy-footed chairs,
A glass bell loaded with wax grapes and pears,

A polished table, holding down the look
Of bracket, mantelpiece, and marbled book.

Staying within the cluttered square of fact,
I cannot slip the clumsy fond contact:

So step into the corridor and start,
Directed by the compass of my heart.

II

Although the narrow corridor appears
So short, the journey took me twenty years.

Each gesture that my habit taught me fell
Down to the boards and made an obstacle.

I paused to watch the fly marks on a shelf,
And found the great obstruction of myself.

I reached the end but, pacing back and forth,
I could not see what reaching it was worth.

In corridors the rooms are undefined:
I groped to feel a handle in the mind.

Testing my faculties I found a stealth
Of passive illness lurking in my health.

And though I saw the corridor stretch bare,
Dusty, and hard, I doubted it was there;

Doubted myself, what final evidence
Lay in perceptions or in common sense?

III

My cause lay in the will, that opens straight
Upon an act for the most desperate.

That simple handle found, I entered in
The other room, where I had never been.

I found within it heavy-footed chairs,
A glass bell loaded with wax grapes and pears,

A polished table, holding down the look
Of bracket, mantelpiece, and marbled book.

Much like the first, this room in which I went.
Only my being there is different.

At the Back of the North Wind

All summer's warmth was stored there in the hay;
Below, the troughs of water froze: the boy
Climbed nightly up the rungs behind the stalls
And planted deep between the clothes he heard
The kind wind bluster, but the last he knew
Was sharp and filled his head, the smell of hay.

Here wrapped within the cobbled mews he woke.
Passing from summer, climbing down through winter
He broke into an air that kept no season:
Denying change, for it was always there.
It nipped the memory numb, scalding away
The castle of winter and the smell of hay.

The ostlers knew, but did not tell him more
Than hay is what we turn to. Other smells,
Horses, leather, manure, fresh sweat, and sweet
Mortality, he found them on the North.
That was her sister, East, that shrilled all day
And swept the mews dead clean from wisps of hay.

Before the Carnival

A painting by Carl Timner

Look, in the attic, the unentered room,
A naked boy leans on the outspread knees
Of his tall brother lolling in costume,
Tights, vest, and cap, of one who on trapeze
Finds comfort farthest from complacencies.

Behind the little boy and acrobat
Through circling half-light from their downshed musing
Hurries the miser in his double hat;
The dry guitar he holds is still, abusing
All others who play music of their choosing.

And lit by a sudden artificial beam
A smocked pretender with his instrument,
Knowing that he is fragment of a dream,
Smirks none the less with borrowed merriment
And twangs for approbation from the front.

Why should they listen when he sings about
The joy of others that he cannot share?
A sexual gossip with a doll-like pout
He cannot touch the objects of his stare:
A prodigal's reflections swimming there.

The boy, his brother's hand upon his arm,
Sees neither where the lava flow of chance
Overtook habit, for he feels the palm
Of him whose turning muscle's nonchalance
Transforms to clockwork their prepared advance.

He too must pick an instrument at length
For this is painted during carnival:
Shall it be then a simple rung of strength
Or these with many strings where well-trained skill
May touch one while it keeps the others still?

And both must dress for the trooping, but the man
Is yet too active and the boy too young
For cloak or fur of heavy thought. They scan
The pace of silence, by the dancers shown
Robes of bright scarlet, horns that were never blown.

Rome

Human Condition

Now it is fog, I walk
Contained within my coat;
No castle more cut off
By reason of its moat:
Only the sentry's cough,
The mercenaries' talk.

The street lamps, visible,
Drop no light on the ground,
But press beams painfully
In a yard of fog around.
I am condemned to be
An individual.

In the established border
There balances a mere
Pinpoint of consciousness.
I stay, or start from, here:
No fog makes more or less
The neighbouring disorder.

Particular, I must
Find out the limitation
Of mind and universe,
To pick thought and sensation
And turn to my own use
Disordered hate or lust.

I seek, to break, my span.
I am my one touchstone.
This is a test more hard
Than any ever known.

And thus I keep my guard
On that which makes me man.

Much is unknowable.
No problem shall be faced
Until the problem is;
I, born to fog, to waste,
Walk through hypothesis,
An individual.

A Plan of Self Subjection

A fragment of weak flesh that circles round
Between the sky and the hot crust of hell,
I circle because I have found
That tracing circles is a useful spell
Against contentment, which comes on by stealth;
Because I have found that from the heaven sun
Can scorch like hell itself,
I end my circle where I had begun.

I put this pen to paper and my verse
Imposes form upon my fault described
So that my fault is worse –
Not from condonement but from being bribed
With order: and with this it appears strong,
Which lacks all order that it can exist.
Yet before very long
From poem back to original I twist.

As Alexander or Mark Antony
Or Coriolanus, whom I most admire,
I mask self-flattery.
And yet however much I may aspire
I stay myself – no perfect king or lover
Or stoic. Even this becomes unreal.
Each tainted with the other
Becomes diseased, both self and self's ideal.

In sex do I not dither more than either
In verse or pose, does not the turncoat sense
Show itself slicker, lither
In changing sides according to the hints

That hopes give out, or action seems to breathe?
Here is most shade my longing, from the sun
And that hot hell beneath.
My circle's end is where I have begun.

Birthday Poem

You understand both Adolphe and Fabrice
    The speculative man or passionate;
You know the smarmies, but side-step the grease
    Ably appraising depth, direction, rate;
Through narrow seas you plunge, to seek the Fleece,
    So sure, you even risk arriving late,
    By flirting, hook-wise, with attractive bait.

You teach Adolphe a hair-raising escape
    Out of the round cell of his lover's eyes,
Show him a huge world with a violent shape;
    You teach Fabrice to sit and analyse;
The smart are dead waist-down: you wear no crêpe;
    You leave the mermaid, having formed no ties;
    You get the Golden Fleece, you are so wise.

Yet you for all the sanity and ease,
    The disconcerting smile omniscient,
Are prisoned in perplexity like these,
    Fabrice and Adolphe; on your discontent
An ailing parasite; to enemies,
    Ponces and whores, concede, because intent
    On groping round your own bewilderment.

First Meeting with a Possible Mother-in-law

She thought, without the benefit of knowing,
You, who had been hers, were not any more.
We had locked our love in to leave nothing showing
From the room her handiwork had crammed before;
But – much revealing in its figured sewing –
A piece of stuff hung out, caught in the door.
I caused the same suspicion I watched growing:
Who could not tell what whole the part stood for?

There was small likeness between her and me:
Two strangers left upon a bare top landing,
I for a prudent while, she totally.

But, eyes turned from the bright material hint,
Each shared too long a second's understanding,
Learning the other's terms of banishment.

Autumn Chapter in a Novel

Through woods, Mme Une Telle, a trifle ill
With idleness, but no less beautiful,
Walks with the young tutor, round their feet
Mob syllables slurred to a fine complaint,
Which in their time held off the natural heat.

The sun is distant, and they fill out space
Sweatless as watercolour under glass.
He kicks abruptly. But we may suppose
The leaves he scatters thus will settle back
In much the same position as they rose.

A tutor's indignation works on air,
Altering nothing; action bustles where,
Towards the pool by which they lately stood,
The husband comes discussing with his bailiff
Poachers, the broken fences round the wood.

Pighead! The poacher is at large, and lingers,
A dead mouse gripped between his sensitive fingers:
Fences already keep the live game out:
See how your property twists her parasol,
Hesitates in the tender trap of doubt.

Here they repair, here daily handle lightly
The brief excitements that disturb them nightly;
Sap draws back inch by inch, and to the ground
The words they uttered rustle constantly:
Silent, they watch the growing, weightless mound.

They leave at last a chosen element,
Resume the motions of their discontent;

She takes her sewing up, and he again
Names to her son the deserts on the globe,
And leaves thrust violently upon the pane.

The Wheel of Fortune

Strapped helpless, monarchs and prelates, round they swung.
O mutability they cried, O perfect Wheel!
    The bishop dreamt of ruin while he dozed,
    A lover that his secrets were exposed,
And Lambert Simnel that he stirred the king's porridge.

Deeper they dream, disorder comes: high, low, are flung
Faster, limbs spinning. As the great Hub cracks they peel
    From off the Felloe of that even round.
    Bishop and lover sprawl upon the ground,
And Lambert Simnel stirs the under footman's porridge.

The Silver Age

Do not enquire from the centurion nodding
At the corner, with his head gentle over
The swelling breastplate, where true Rome is found.
Even of Livy there are volumes lost.
All he can do is guide you through the moonlight.

When he moves, mark how his eager striding,
To which we know the darkness is a river
Sullen with mud, is easy as on ground.
We know it is a river never crossed
By any but some few who hate the moonlight.

And when he speaks, mark how his ancient wording
Is hard with indignation of a lover.
'I do not think our new Emperor likes the sound
Of turning squadrons or the last post.
Consorts with Christians, I think he lives in moonlight.'

Hurrying to show you his companions guarding,
He grips your arm like a cold strap of leather,
Then halts, earthpale, as he stares round and round.
What made this one fragment of a sunken coast
Remain, far out, to be beaten by the moonlight?

The Unsettled Motorcyclist's Vision of his Death

Across the open countryside,
Into the walls of rain I ride.
It beats my cheek, drenches my knees,
But I am being what I please.

The firm heath stops, and marsh begins.
Now we're at war: whichever wins
My human will cannot submit
To nature, though brought out of it.
The wheels sink deep; the clear sound blurs:
Still, bent on the handle-bars,
I urge my chosen instrument
Against the mere embodiment.
The front wheel wedges fast between
Two shrubs of glazed insensate green
– Gigantic order in the rim
Of each flat leaf. Black eddies brim
Around my heel which, pressing deep,
Accelerates the waiting sleep.

I used to live in sound, and lacked
Knowledge of still or creeping fact,
But now the stagnant strips my breath,
Leant on my cheek in weight of death.
Though so oppressed I find I may
Through substance move. I pick my way,
Where death and life in one combine,
Through the dark earth that is not mine,
Crowded with fragments, blunt, unformed;
While past my ear where noises swarmed
The marsh plant's white extremities,

Slow without patience, spread at ease
Invulnerable and soft, extend
With a quiet grasping toward their end.

And though the tubers, once I rot,
Reflesh my bones with pallid knot,
Till swelling out my clothes they feign
This dummy is a man again,
It is as servants they insist,
Without volition that they twist;
And habit does not leave them tired,
By men laboriously acquired.
Cell after cell the plants convert
My special richness in the dirt:
All that they get, they get by chance.

And multiply in ignorance.

Lines for a Book

I think of all the toughs through history
And thank heaven they lived, continually.
I praise the overdogs from Alexander
To those who would not play with Stephen Spender.
Their pride exalted some, some overthrew,
But was not vanity at last: they knew
That though the mind has also got a place
It's not in marvelling at its mirrored face
And evident sensibility. It's better
To go and see your friend than write a letter;
To be a soldier than to be a cripple;
To take an early weaning from the nipple
Than think your mother is the only girl;
To be insensitive, to steel the will,
Than sit irresolute all day at stool
Inside the heart; and to despise the fool,
Who may not help himself and may not choose,
Than give him pity which he cannot use.
I think of those exclusive by their action,
For whom mere thought could be no satisfaction –
The athletes lying under tons of dirt
Or standing gelded so they cannot hurt
The pale curators and the families
By calling up disturbing images.
I think of all the toughs through history
And thank heaven they lived, continually.

Elvis Presley

Two minutes long it pitches through some bar:
Unreeling from a corner box, the sigh
Of this one, in his gangling finery
And crawling sideburns, wielding a guitar.

The limitations where he found success
Are ground on which he, panting, stretches out
In turn, promiscuously, by every note.
Our idiosyncrasy and our likeness.

We keep ourselves in touch with a mere dime:
Distorting hackneyed words in hackneyed songs
He turns revolt into a style, prolongs
The impulse to a habit of the time.

Whether he poses or is real, no cat
Bothers to say: the pose held is a stance,
Which, generation of the very chance
It wars on, may be posture for combat.

Market at Turk

At the street corner, hunched up,
he gestates action, prepared
for some unique combat in
boots, jeans, and a curious cap
whose very peak, jammed forward,
indicates resolution.

It is military, almost,
how he buckles himself in,
with bootstraps and Marine belt,
reminders of the will, lest
even with that hard discipline
the hardness should not be felt.

He waits, whom no door snatches
to unbuckling in the close
commotion of bar or bed,
he presides in apartness,
not yet knowing his purpose
fully, and fingers the blade.

In Praise of Cities

I

Indifferent to the indifference that conceived her,
Grown buxom in disorder now, she accepts
– Like dirt, strangers, or moss upon her churches –
Your tribute to the wharf of circumstance,
Rejected sidestreet, formal monument ...
And, irresistible, the thoroughfare.

You welcome in her what remains of you;
And what is strange and what is incomplete
Compels a passion without understanding,
For all you cannot be.

II

Only at dawn
You might escape, she sleeps then for an hour:
Watch where she hardly breathes, spread out and cool,
Her pavements desolate in the dim dry air.

III

You stay. Yet she is occupied, apart.
Out of a mist the river turns to see
Whether you follow still. You stay. At evening
Your blood gains pace even as her blood does.

IV

Casual yet urgent in her love making,
She constantly asserts her independence:

Suddenly turning moist pale walls upon you
– Your own designs, peeling and unachieved –
Or her whole darkness hunching in an alley.
And all at once you enter the embrace
Withheld by day while you solicited.
She wanders lewdly, whispering her given name,
Charing Cross Road, or Forty-Second Street:
The longest streets, desire that never ends,
Familiar and inexplicable, wearing
Cosmetic light a fool could penetrate.
She presses you with her hard ornaments,
Arcades, late movie shows, the piled lit windows
Of surplus stores. Here she is loveliest;
Extreme, material, and the work of man.

The Allegory of the Wolf Boy

The causes are in Time; only their issue
Is bodied in the flesh, the finite powers.
And how to guess he hides in that firm tissue
Seeds of division? At tennis and at tea
Upon the gentle lawn, he is not ours,
But plays us in a sad duplicity.

Tonight the boy, still boy open and blond,
Breaks from the house, wedges his clothes between
Two moulded garden urns, and goes beyond
His understanding, through the dark and dust:
Fields of sharp stubble, abandoned by machine
To the whirring enmity of insect lust.

As yet ungolden in the dense, hot night
The spikes enter his feet: he seeks the moon,
Which, with the touch of its infertile light,
Shall loose desires hoarded against his will
By the long urging of the afternoon.
Slowly the hard rim shifts above the hill.

White in the beam he stops, faces it square
And the same instant leaping from the ground
Feels the familiar itch of close dark hair;
Then, clean exception to the natural laws,
Only to instinct and the moon being bound,
Drops on four feet. Yet he has bleeding paws.

The Beaters

'None but my foe to be my guide.'

I

I see them careful, choosing limitation,
And careful still to break their loneliness
Only for one who, perfect counterpart,
Welcomes the tools of their perversity,
Whip, cords, and strap, and toiling toward despair
Can feel the pain sweet, tranquil, in his blood.

II

And what appear the dandy's affectation
– The swastika-draped bed, or links that press
In twined and gleaming weight beneath a shirt –
Are emblems to recall identity;
Through violent parables their special care
Is strictly to explore that finitude.

III

For in that discipline of resignation
Each gesture is deliberate: they confess
A manacled desire, and this resort
Both limits and implies their liberty.
Ambiguous liberty! it is the air
Between the raised arm and the fallen thud.

IV

Some loose the object of their devastation,
To raise him with an ultimate gentleness,

[26]

A candid touch where formerly they hurt.
It was no end, merely extremity.
They know they shall resume pursuit, elsewhere,
Of what they would not hold to if they could.

V

The lips that meet the wound can finally
Justify nothing — neither pain nor care;
Tender upon the shoulders ripe with blood.

Julian the Apostate

Lictor or heavy slave would wear it best,
The robe of uncapricious Emperor,
Waging a profitable war, at least
Knowing rule lay in gathered fold, not them.
But Julian bursts the doubly sacred hem;
Weighted enough by every growing hair.

Born in mid progress of his history
He is perceptive of the sudden wrong
In those deliberate laws he framed today:
The absolute is hard to formulate:
Failure, desire, seek out their man; the date
Is relative, they die once they belong.

High in the palace, his concern is more
With a spirit self-created but cross-bred.
He sees them gather, reach the great church door,
Waving red flowers; from it frost: the bands
Of monks emerge with axes in their hands.
They swim among the pagans, white on red.

No subject can divert his cold resolve
To fix a question that, eluding name,
To make corporeal would be to solve.
The answer lies in some embodiment
Of question mark itself, not what is meant:
He stoops within that hypothetical frame.

Then strains to lift his bones erect, and fling
To the pure will of exclamation mark
In the discovered or discovering.

At length he pulls the only exclamation
Complete towards him, his assassination;
And greets an outrage of the simpler dark.

Jesus and his Mother

My only son, more God's than mine,
Stay in this garden ripe with pears.
The yielding of their substance wears
A modest and contented shine:
And when they weep with age, not brine
But lazy syrup are their tears.
'I am my own and not my own.'

He seemed much like another man,
That silent foreigner who trod
Outside my door with lily rod:
How could I know what I began
Meeting the eyes more furious than
The eyes of Joseph, those of God?
I was my own and not my own.

And who are these twelve labouring men?
I do not understand your words:
I taught you speech, we named the birds,
You marked their big migrations then
Like any child. So turn again
To silence from the place of crowds.
'I am my own and not my own.'

Why are you sullen when I speak?
Here are your tools, the saw and knife
And hammer on your bench. Your life
Is measured here in week and week
Planed as the furniture you make,
And I will teach you like a wife
To be my own and all my own.

Who like an arrogant wind blown
Where he may please, needs no content?
Yet I remember how you went
To speak with scholars in furred gown.
I hear an outcry in the town;
Who carried that dark instrument?
'One all his own and not his own.'

Treading the green and nimble sward
I stare at a strange shadow thrown.
Are you the boy I bore alone,
No doctor near to cut the cord?
I cannot reach to call you Lord,
Answer me as my only son.
'I am my own and not my own.'

St Martin and the Beggar

Martin sat young upon his bed
A budding cenobite,
Said 'Though I hold the principles
Of Christian life be right,
I cannot grow from them alone,
I must go out to fight.'

He travelled hard, he travelled far,
The light began to fail.
'Is not this act of mine,' he said,
'A cowardly betrayal,
Should I not peg my nature down
With a religious nail?'

Wind scudded on the marshland,
And, dangling at his side,
His sword soon clattered under hail:
What could he do but ride? –
There was not shelter for a dog,
The garrison far ahead.

A ship that moves on darkness
He road across the plain,
When a brawny beggar started up
Who pulled at his rein
And leant dripping with sweat and water
Upon the horse's mane.

He glared into Martin's eyes
With eyes more wild than bold;
His hair sent rivers down his spine;
Like a fowl plucked to be sold

His flesh was grey. Martin said –
'What, naked in this cold?'

'I have no food to give you,
Money would be a joke.'
Pulling his new sword from the sheath
He took his soldier's cloak
And cut it in two equal parts
With a single stroke.

Grabbing one to his shoulders,
Pinning it with his chin,
The beggar dived into the dark,
And soaking to the skin
Martin went on slowly
Until he reached an inn.

One candle on the wooden table,
The food and drink were poor,
The woman hobbled off, he ate,
Then casually before
The table stood the beggar as
If he had used the door.

Now dry for hair and flesh had been
By warm airs fanned,
Still bare but round each muscled thigh
A single golden band,
His eyes now wild with love, he held
The half cloak in his hand.

'You recognised the human need
Included yours, because
You did not hesitate, my saint,
To cut your cloak across;

But never since that moment
Did you regret the loss.

'My enemies would have turned away,
My holy toadies would
Have given all the cloak and frozen
Conscious that they were good.
But you, being a saint of men,
Gave only what you could.'

St Martin stretched his hand out
To offer from his plate,
But the beggar vanished, thinking food
Like cloaks is needless weight.
Pondering on the matter,
St Martin bent and ate.

To Yvor Winters, 1955

I leave you in your garden.
                              In the yard
Behind it, run the airedales you have reared
With boxer's vigilance and poet's rigour:
Dog-generations you have trained the vigour
That few can breed to train and fewer still
Control with the deliberate human will.
And in the house there rest, piled shelf on shelf,
The accumulations that compose the self –
Poem and history: for if we use
Words to maintain the actions that we choose,
Our words, with slow defining influence,
Stay to mark out our chosen lineaments.

Continual temptation waits on each
To renounce his empire over thought and speech,
Till he submit his passive faculties
To evening, come where no resistance is;
The unmotivated sadness of the air
Filling the human with his own despair.
Where now lies power to hold the evening back?
Implicit in the grey is total black:
Denial of the discriminating brain
Brings the neurotic vision, and the vein
Of necromancy. All as relative
For mind as for the sense, we have to live
In a half-world, not ours nor history's,
And learn the false from half-true premisses.

But sitting in the dusk – though shapes combine,
Vague mass replacing edge and flickering line,

[35]

You keep both Rule and Energy in view,
Much power in each, most in the balanced two:
Ferocity existing in the fence
Built by an exercised intelligence.
Though night is always close, complete negation
Ready to drop on wisdom and emotion,
Night from the air or the carnivorous breath,
Still it is right to know the force of death,
And, as you do, persistent, tough in will,
Raise from the excellent the better still.

The Inherited Estate

To Mike Kitay, an American in Europe

A mansion, string of cottages, a farm,
Before you reach the last black-timbered barn
And set your foot upon the path that leads
Up to the hill where Follies and façades
– Typical products of intelligence
That lacks brute purpose – split, disintegrate,
   And, falling with their own rich weight,
Litter the slopes, a record of expense.

So generations of the reckless dead
Put up the ruins you inherited,
And generations of ganged village boys
Have used as fort and ammunition those
Droppings of fashion you explore today.
What country boys and gentlemen have left
   Now smells of green, the fat dark drift
Where the weed's impulse couples with decay.

Is comfort so impermanently built,
A summer house with blurring fungus split
At random on the leaning walls? is time
Only a carved head that you fish from slime,
That winks with muddied eyeball? does the crash
Of failing stonework sound for all desires?
   For, once the dilettante tires,
The ornaments he raises fall in trash.

A calm discrimination marks your hate:
Once you inherited the wide estate
The Follies like the land and farm were yours.

Distance has flattered them, for from the moors
The fronts resembled solid palaces:
And though you are not so trusting to believe
    That all is sound which others leave,
You come not crediting half your bailiff says.

He told you all, an honest labourer.
But had not noticed this, that in the year
When you were born a twist of feckless wind
Brought one small seed and left it on the ground
Between the chance and choice to live or die.
It drew the means of living undeterred,
    Uncurling in the shell it stirred,
To rise, and sway upon your property.

Its art is merely holding to the earth —
But see how confidently, from its birth,
Its branches, lifting above failures, keep
Vigour within the discipline of shape.
Come here, friend, yearly, till you've carved the bark
With all the old virtues, young in fibre, names
    That swell with time and tree, no dreams,
No ornaments, but tallies for your work.

During an Absence

I used to think that obstacles to love
   Were out of date, the darkened stairs
Leading deprived ones to the mossy tomb
Where she lay carpeted with golden hairs:
   We had no place in such a room,
Belonging to the common ground above.

In sunlight we are free to move, and hold
   Our open assignations, yet
Each love defines its proper obstacles:
Our frowning Montague and Capulet
   Are air, not individuals
And have no faces for their frowns to fold.

Even in sunlight what does freedom mean?
   Romeo's passion rose to fire
From one thin spark within a brace of days.
We for whom time draws out, visas expire,
   Smoulder without a chance to blaze
Upon the unities of a paper scene.

The violence of a picturesque account
   Gives way to details, none the less
Reaching, each one more narrow than the last,
Down to a separate hygienic place
   Where acting love is in the past,
No golden hairs are there, no bleeding count.

No, if there were bright things to fasten on
   There'd be no likeness to the play.
But under a self-generated glare

Any bad end has possibility,
    The means endurance. I declare
I know how hard upon the ground it shone.

The Separation

Must we for ever eye through space? and make
Contact too much for comfort and yet less,
Like Peter Quint and that strange governess
Divided by a window or a lake?
Deprived like ghost, like man, both glare, then move
Apart in shadow. Must the breath swim between,
The trampled meadow of words yet intervene,
To part desire from the tall muscle of love?
I thought, that night, the evening of the tower,
When I could almost touch you, you were so clear,
That I was Quint and it was all the rest
Kept you away, the children or the hour;

But now you prowl in the garden and I am here,
What dead charge do I pull upon my breast?

High Fidelity

I play your furies back to me at night,
The needle dances in the grooves they made,
For fury is passion like love, and fury's bite,
These grooves, no sooner than a love mark fade;
Then all swings round to nightmare: from the rim,
To prove the guilt I don't admit by day,
I duck love as a witch to sink or swim
Till in the ringed and level I survey
The tuneless circles that succeed a voice.
They run, without distinction, passion, rage,
Around a soloist's merely printed name
That still turns, from the impetus not choice,
Surrounded in that played-out pose of age
By notes he was, but cannot be again.

Legal Reform

Condemned to life, a happier condemnation
Than I deserved, I serve my sentence full,
Clasping it to me at each indication
That this time love is not the paradox
By which, whatever it contains, my cell
Contains the absolute, because it locks.

It all led up to this, a simple law
Passed by ourselves, which holds me in its power.
Not till I stopped the theft of all I saw
Just for the having's sake, could it be passed.
Now I refer disposal of each hour
To this, a steady precedent at last.

My sentence stipulated exercise
Painful and lonely in the walks of death
With twittering clouds of spirits; still there lies
Beneath the common talk my single hope:
I must get back inside the cage of breath
For absence twitches on the loosened rope.

Marched off to happiness, I quarry stone
Hour after hour, and sweat my past away.
Already I have made, working alone,
Notable excavations, and the guard,
Turning desire, who eyes me all the day,
Has no use for his whip, I work so hard.

Condemned to hope, to happiness, to life,
Condemned to shift in your enclosing eyes,
I soon correct those former notions rife

Among the innocent, or fetter-maimed.
For law is in our hands, I realise:
The sentence is, condemned to be condemned.

Puss in Boots to the Giant

In fine simplicity
I cry On either side
Far as the eye can see
These fields as green as wide
Are my master's property.

The cattle browze their fill,
All day the tall boys sweat
With the bags in the mill,
And after sun set
Jack has his Jill.

And then upon the grass
How lasting and how clean
Without token alas
They banish the lean
Highway beggars that pass.

It is not selfishness
But when they enjoy
Two triumphs in one place
Every girl and boy
Like the defeated less.

So praise the pitiless, hot
In each other's arms.
Gigglers, gossips, do not
Come near. You, Itching Palms,
We condemn to Thought.

In fine simplicity
I cry On either side

Far as the eye can see
These fields as green as wide
Are my master's property.

Thoughts on Unpacking

Unpacking in the raw new rooms, I clear,
Or try to clear, a space for us, that we
May cultivate an ease of moving here
   With no encumbrance near,
In amplitude. But something hinders me:

Where do these go, these knick-knacks I forgot?
– Gadgets we bought and kept, thinking perhaps
They might be useful some day, and a lot
   Of others that were not:
Bent keys, Italian grammars, Mickey Mouse caps.

And there are worse grotesques that, out of sight,
Unpacked, unlabelled, somehow followed too:
The urgencies we did not share, the spite
   Of such and such a night,
Poses, mistakes – an unclean residue –

That drift, one after other, till I find
They have filled the space I carefully prepared;
The sagging shapes I thought we left behind
   Crawl out within the mind
Seeming to sneer 'This is the past you shared.'

I take a broom to them; but when I thrust
Round the diminished luggage, some roll back,
Surviving from my outbreak of disgust
   As balls of hair and dust
Made buoyant with a kind of fictive lack.

I need your help with these. They rest unseen
In furniture we know, and plot a changing

To grey confusion of the space between.
Now, as I sweep it clean,
I realise that love is an arranging.

Merlin in the Cave: He Speculates without a Book

This was the end and yet, another start:
Held by the arms of lust from lust I pace
About the dim fulfilment of my art,
Impatient in the flesh I eye a space
Where, warlock, once I might have left this place,
A form of life my tool, creeping across
The shelving rock as rank convolvulus.

The Rock. The space, too narrow for a hand.
Pressing my head between two slopes of stone
I peer at what I do not understand,
The movement: clouds, and separate rooks blown
Back on their flight. Where do they fly, alone?
I lost their instinct. It was late. To me
The bird is only meat for augury.

And here the mauve convolvulus falls in,
Its narrow stalk as fat and rich in sap
As I was rich in lusting to begin
A life I could have had and finished up
Years, years before. With aphrodisiac
I brought back vigour; oiled and curled my hair;
Reduced my huge obesity, to wear

The green as tightly girdled at my waist
As any boy who leapt about the court;
And with an unguent I made my chest
Fit for the iron plate. I still held short
Of wrestling as the boys did: from their sport
They slid back panting on the tiles to look
At one distinguished now by scent, not book.

Love was a test: I was all-powerful,
So failed, because I let no fault intrude.
A philosophic appetite. By rule
I calculated each fond attitude
But those that self-distrust makes more than mood,
The quick illogical motions, negative
But evidence that lovers move and live.

I watch the flux I never guessed: the grass;
The watchful animal that gnaws a root,
Knowing possession means the risk of loss;
Ripeness that rests an hour in the fruit.
Yet locked here with the very absolute
I challenged, I must try to break the hold:
This cave is empty, and is very cold.

I must grow back through knowledge, passing it
Like casual landmarks in a well-known land,
Great mausoleums over ancient wit,
Doors that would swing at my complacent hand;
And come at last, being glad to understand
The touched, the seen, and only those, to where
I find the earth is suddenly black and near.

And having reached the point where there remain
No knacks or habits, and these empty cells
Are matched by a great emptiness in my brain:
Unhampered by remembered syllables,
The youth I wasted at precocious spells
Will grow upon me, and my wants agree
In the sweet promiscuity of the bee.

And yet, the danger. All within my mind
Hovers complete, and if it never grows
It never rots; for what I leave behind

Contains no fight within itself: the rose
Is full and drops no petal, emblems doze
Perfect and quiet as if engraved in books,
Not like the fighting boys and wind-torn rooks.

The bee's world and the rook's world are the same:
Where clouds do, or do not, let through the light;
Too mixed, unsimple, for a simple blame;
Belligerent: but no one starts the fight,
And nothing ends it but a storm or night.
Alchemists, only, boil away the pain,
And pick out value as one small dry grain.

And turned upon the flooding relative,
What could I do but start the quest once more
Towards the terrible cave in which I live,
The absolute prison where chance thrust me before
I built it round me on my study floor;
What could I do but seek the synthesis
As each man does, of what his nature is?

Knowing the end to movement, I will shrink
From movement not for its own wilful sake.
– How can a man live, and not act or think
Without an end? But I must act, and make
The meaning in each movement that I take.
Rook, bee, you are the whole and not a part.
This is an end, and yet another start.

The Corridor

A separate place between the thought and felt
The empty hotel corridor was dark.
But here the keyhole shone, a meaning spark.
What fires were latent in it! So he knelt.

Now, at the corridor's much lighter end,
A pierglass hung upon the wall and showed,
As by an easily deciphered code,
Dark, door, and man, hooped by a single band.

He squinted through the keyhole, and within
Surveyed an act of love that frank as air
He was too ugly for, or could not dare,
Or at a crucial moment thought a sin.

Pleasure was simple thus: he mastered it.
If once he acted as participant
He would be mastered, the inhabitant
Of someone else's world, mere shred to fit.

He moved himself to get a better look
And then it was he noticed in the glass
Two strange eyes in a fascinated face
That watched him like a picture in a book.

The instant drove simplicity away –
The scene was altered, it depended on
His kneeling, when he rose they were clean gone
The couple in the keyhole; this would stay.

For if the watcher of the watcher shown
There in the distant glass, should be watched too,

Who can be master, free of others; who
Can look around and say he is alone?

Moreover, who can know that what he sees
Is not distorted, that he is not seen
Distorted by a pierglass, curved and lean?
Those curious eyes, through him, were linked to these –

These lovers altered in the cornea's bend.
What could he do but leave the keyhole, rise,
Holding those eyes as equal in his eyes,
And go, one hand held out, to meet a friend?

Vox Humana

Being without quality
I appear to you at first
as an unkempt smudge, a blur,
an indefinite haze, mere-
ly pricking the eyes, almost
nothing. Yet you perceive me.

I have been always most close
when you had least resistance,
falling asleep, or in bars;
during the unscheduled hours,
though strangely without substance,
I hang, there and ominous.

Aha, sooner or later
you will have to name me, and,
as you name, I shall focus,
I shall become more precise.
O Master (for you command
in naming me, you prefer)!

I was, for Alexander,
the certain victory; I
was hemlock for Socrates;
and, in the dry night, Brutus
waking before Philippi
stopped me, crying out 'Caesar!'

Or if you call me the blur
that in fact I am, you shall
yourself remain blurred, hanging

like smoke indoors. For you bring,
to what you define now, all
there is, ever, of future.